Bull D

Written by Jill Eggleton
Illustrated by Sandra Cammell

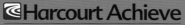

Harcourt Achieve
Rigby · Saxon · Steck-Vaughn

www.HarcourtAchieve.com
1.800.531.5015

As a kid, I was always scared of the big black bull we had on our farm.

I was terrified when he tossed his head and pawed the ground, making the dirt fly into the sky.

My father told my brother and me that bulls couldn't always be trusted. That they didn't like anything to come near their "flight zone."

"Their flight zone is their safety zone," he said. "Bulls can get upset if something enters their flight zone."

My brother acted big and tough around the bull. He said he wasn't scared of it at all and that I was just a wimp, a wuss, a scaredy pants!

3

One day I was watching the bull when my brother said, "I dare you to walk across the paddock."

"No way," I said.

"The bull won't even see you," he told me. "You could prove you're not a wimp!"

I looked at the bull. It did seem calm. Maybe he wouldn't notice me. I felt a surge of braveness wash over me *like a big wave.*

"I'll give you my chocolate bar," said my brother.

"Not enough," I said. "I want the chocolate bar and your new marker pens."

My brother thought for a minute. Then he shook my hand. "It's a deal," he said.

I was really scared, but I crawled under the fence and slowly walked across the paddock. I kept close to the fence line.

My heart was beating loudly in my chest, but the bull paid no attention to me.

I got to the other side feeling very pleased with myself.

"You can't call me a wimp now!" I shouted at my brother.

But my brother laughed. "That was easy," he said. "The real test is to walk across the paddock in my red jacket. That is a true test of bravery. If you can do that, I will never call you a wimp again."

Now my brother was being really mean. He'd always told me that bulls don't like red.

I looked at the bull. He hadn't moved one bit.

Suddenly I felt brave and bold. "I'll do it," I said, "if you give me your robot lamp."

I loved my brother's robot lamp. It had three lights on long silver arms that could move anywhere.

"No!" said my brother. "You can't have my lamp."

8

But I wanted that lamp more than anything, and I was feeling really brave now.

"What if I go across the middle of the paddock?" I asked.

My brother grinned. "OK," he said. "It's a deal."

9

I put on my brother's red jacket and crawled under the fence. My heart was beating loudly again - **like bongo drums** this time.

I started to walk across the paddock. I was a long way from the fence.

Then, to my horror, I saw the bull lower his head and come charging straight toward me.

I panicked.

I started to run, but I tripped on the rough ground and fell flat on my face.

I lay there, frozen in fear.

Then I saw my father in the paddock, waving a broom. Our dogs were following him, yapping and snapping at the bull. The bull turned his head for a moment.

My mind unfroze. I jumped to my feet and ran *like a flash of lightning* across the paddock and under the fence.

My father was very angry when he heard the story.

"Never do something just because someone dares you to," he said. "You could have been killed by that bull."

I knew I had been very silly. I had entered the bull's flight zone!

Later on that day, my brother gave me the new markers and the lamp, but he kept the chocolate bar.

"You had some help," he said.

He did keep his promise, though, and he never called me a wimp, a wuss, or a scaredy pants ever again!

Recounts

Recounts tell about something that has happened.

A recount tells the reader
- what happened
- to whom
- where it happened
- when it happened

A recount tells events in sequence . . .

. . . and has a
conclusion

▬▬ Guide Notes

Title: Bull Dare
Stage: Fluency (2)

Text Form: Recount
Approach: Guided Reading
Processes: Thinking Critically, Exploring Language, Processing Information
Written and Visual Focus: Illustrative Text

THINKING CRITICALLY
(sample questions)
- What do you think this story could be about? Look at the title and discuss.
- Look at the cover. Why do you think the bull is angry?
- Look at pages 2-3. Why do you think the father said that bulls couldn't always be trusted?
- Look at pages 4-5. Why do you think the brother said that the bull wouldn't see the narrator?
- Look at pages 6-7. How do you know that the narrator was really scared?
- Look at pages 10-11. How do you know the bull was not happy?
- Look at pages 8-9. Why do you think the brother grinned?
- Look at pages 12-13. How do you think the brother felt when the narrator fell over? Why do you think this?
- Look at pages 14-15. Why do you think the dogs weren't scared of the bull?
- Look at pages 16-17. Do you think the brother should have kept the chocolate bar? Why do you think this?

EXPLORING LANGUAGE

Terminology
Title, cover, illustrations, author, illustrator

Vocabulary
Clarify: flight zone, wimp, wuss, paddock, bongo, horror, unfroze
Nouns: farm, bull, brother, father, chocolate bar
Verbs: crawled, walk, grinned, lower, tripped
Singular/plural: marker/markers, drum/drums

Print Conventions
Apostrophes – possessives (brother's red jacket, bull's flight zone), contractions (won't, couldn't, didn't, wasn't, it's); abbreviation (OK)